¡Cuéntame!

Student Textbook

A TPRS® Curriculum for Elementary Spanish

Christine Anderson & Valeri Marsh

Illustrated by Justin Greene

Copyright © 2002 by TPRS Publishing, Inc.
P.O. Box 11624
Chandler, AZ 85248
800-TPRISFUN
Info@tprstorytelling.com
www.tprstorytelling.com

¡Cuéntame!

Las aventuras de Gabi

episodio #1

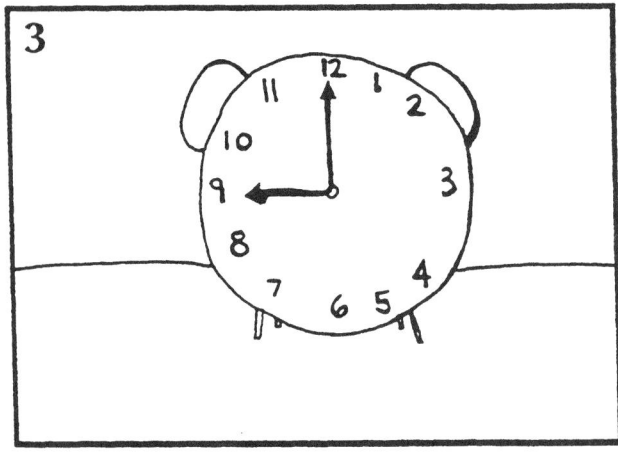

✓ *Exercise #1*
Practice telling episode #1. Use all of the words from the list below.

el lunes	duerme	suena
la gatita	(está) contento/contenta	come
se llama	el despertador	¡Qué problema!

✓ *Exercise #2*
Your teacher will read six sentences describing different pictures from episode #1. Listen to each sentence. Then decide which picture is being described, and write the number of that picture in the appropriate space.

1. _____   4. _____

2. _____   5. _____

3. _____   6. _____

✓ *Exercise #3*
Complete the following sentences with the word or words which make the sentence true.

1. Hay una _____.

2. La gatita _____ Gabi.

3. El lunes Gabi _____.

4. Gabi come _____ y ahora

   está muy _____.

3

✓ *Exercise #4*
Answer the following questions about episode #1.

1. ¿Qué día es?

2. ¿Cómo se llama la gatita?

3. ¿Qué hace la gatita?

4. ¿Cuál es el problema?

5. ¿Cuál es la solución?

✓ *Exercise #5*
Choose any two pictures from episode #1, and narrate them below.

Picture#   *Narration*

_____   _____

            _____

            _____

_____   _____

            _____

            _____

✓ *Exercise #6*
You will hear four questions about episode #1. After you hear each question, read the three possible answers and circle the best answer.

1. a. Sí, es lunes.

    b. No, no es lunes.

    c. No, es martes.

2. a. Es un despertador.

    b. Es una gatita.

    c. Gabi está contenta.

3. a. Porque duerme.

    b. Porque come el despertador.

    c. Porque el despertador suena.

4. a. Gabi no está contenta.

    b. Gabi no duerme.

    c. Gabi duerme más.

Exercise #7
The sentences below are false. Change each sentence to make it true.

1. Hay dos gatitas.

2. La gatita se llama Chela.

3. Gabi suena.

4. El despertador come a Gabi.

5. Cuando el despertador suena, Gabi está contenta.

6. El despertador duerme.

episodio #2

✓ Exercise #8

Practice telling episode #2. Use all of the words from the new vocabulary listed below.

el martes	la criada	se duerme
la aspiradora	prende	otra vez
llega	la radio/el radio	¡Qué ruido!

✓ Exercise #9

Your teacher will read six sentences describing different pictures from episode #2. Listen to each sentence. Then decide which picture is being described, and write the number of that picture in the appropriate space.

1. _____   4. _____

2. _____   5. _____

3. _____   6. _____

✓ Exercise #10

Answer the following questions about episode #2.

1. ¿Qué día es hoy?

2. ¿Quién llega?

3. ¿Qué hace la criada?

4. ¿Por qué no está contenta Gabi?

5. ¿Qué come Gabi?

6. ¿Qué hay en el estómago de Gabi?

✓ *Exercise #11*

Look at the pictures below. Tell what is in each picture. Write at least two sentences for each picture. Start each sentence with the word "hay."

1. _____

2. _____

1. _____

2. _____

✓ *Exercise #12*
Your teacher will describe a scene to you. Draw what you hear described.
Include as many details as you can.

✓ *Exercise #13*
Describe the picture you drew above for Exercise #12. Include as many
details as you can. Try to use complete Spanish sentences.

_____

_____

_____

_____

_____

_____

episodio #3

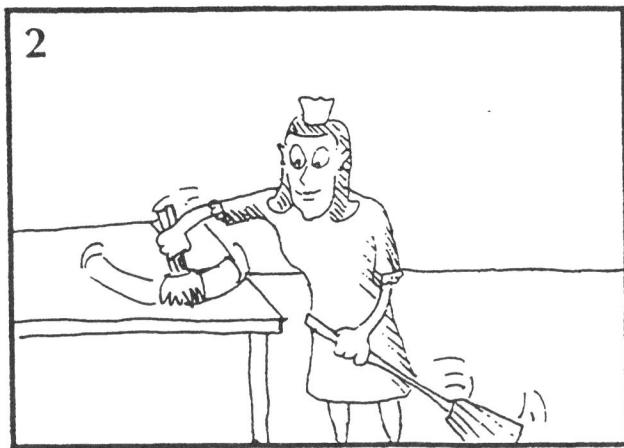

✓ *Exercise #14*
Practice telling episode #3. Use all of the words from the list below.

el miércoles	**limpia**	**la cola**
la casa	**busca**	**pasa la aspiradora**
(está) sucio/sucia	**enchufa**	**¡Qué lío!**

✓ *Exercise #15*
Your teacher will read six sentences describing different pictures from episode #3. Listen to each sentence. Then decide which picture is being described, and write the number of that picture in the appropriate space.

1. _____   4. _____

2. _____   5. _____

3. _____   6. _____

✓ *Exercise #16*
Complete the following sentences with the word or words which make the sentence true.

1. La casa de Gabi está muy _____.

2. La criada _____ la casa.

3. La criada busca la _____.

4. La criada _____ la cola de Gabi.

5. La criada llega a la _____.

✓ *Exercise #17*
You will hear five questions about episode #3. After you hear each question, read the three possible answers and circle the best answer.

1. a. Es lunes.

    b. Es martes.

    c. Es miércoles.

2. a. La criada busca la aspiradora.

    b. Está en el estómago de Gabi.

    c. No hay aspiradora.

3. a. Pasa la aspiradora.

    b. Busca la radio.

    c. Duerme.

4. a. La criada come la cola de Gabi.

    b. La criada enchufa la cola de Gabi.

    c. La criada busca la cola de Gabi.

5. a. Limpia la casa de Gabi.

    b. Limpia la cola de Gabi.

    c. Limpia la aspiradora de Gabi.

✓ *Exercise #18*
Choose any two pictures from episode #3, and narrate them below. Try to add one extra detail, not given in the original story, to each of your narrations.

Picture#   *Narration*

_____   _____

            _____

            _____

_____   _____

            _____

✓ *Exercise #19*

Write the narration for the new mini-story you see illustrated below.

_____

_____

_____

_____

_____

_____

_____

_____

episodio #4

✓ *Exercise #20*
Practice telling episode #4. Use all of the words from the list below.

el jueves	el refrigerador	el imán/los imanes
se pega	cierra	tiene (mucha) hambre
abre	la puerta	¡Qué ridículo!

✓ *Exercise #21*
The sentences below are false. Change each sentence to make it true.

1. Es miércoles.

2. Gabi busca pizza.

3. La criada tiene hambre.

4. Gabi come el refrigerador.

5. Hay chocolate en el refrigerador.

6. Hay chocolate en la puerta del refrigerador.

7. Gabi se pega a la puerta de la casa.

8. La criada cierra la puerta del refrigerador.

✓ *Exercise #22*

Look at the two similar pictures below. Describe how picture #2 differs from picture #1.

1. _____ *Hay dos puertas.* _____

2. _____

3. _____

4. _____

5. _____

6. _____

Exercise #23

You have learned the following four Spanish expressions:

¡Qué problema!   ¡Qué lío!
¡Qué ridículo!   ¡Qué ruido!

You will hear three short situations. After you hear each situation, write the Spanish expression from the list above which would be the best conclusion for the story.

1. _____

2. _____

3. _____

Exercise #24

Listen while your teacher reads the first story from Exercise #23 one more time. Then draw the final scene of the story.

✓ *Exercise #25*
Create an original mini-story using several words from episodes #1-4.
Illustrate and narrate your new story below.

Exercise #26
Choose your favorite episode from #1, #2, #3 or #4 and retell it in the space provided below. Try to add a few extra details that were not given in the original story.

episodio # _____

_____

_____

_____

_____

_____

_____

_____

_____

_____

_____

_____

_____

_____

_____

_____

_____

_____

episodio #5

✓ *Exercise #27*
Practice telling episode #5. Use all of the words from the list below.

la muchacha	**(es) biencriado/biencriada**	**la escuela**
la amiga	**el viernes**	**la nariz**
(es) inteligente	**el examen**	**¡Qué vergüenza!**

✓ *Exercise #28*
Answer the following questions about episode #5.

1. ¿Qué día es hoy?

2. ¿Quién es Marisol?

3. ¿Cómo es Marisol?

4. ¿Por qué es un día importante en la escuela?

5. ¿Cuál es el problema de Marisol?

✓ *Exercise #29*
The sentences below are false. Change each sentence to make it true.

1. La muchacha se llama Paquita.

2. Marisol es estúpida y malcriada.

3. Marisol es una gatita.

4. El martes hay un examen en la escuela.

5. Hay una cola grande en la nariz de Marisol.

21

✓ *Exercise #30*

Choose any two pictures from episode #5, and narrate them below. Add one extra detail, not given in the original story, to each of your narrations.

Picture#   Narration

_____   _____

                    _____

                    _____

_____   _____

                    _____

                    _____

✓ *Exercise #31*

Imagine how Marisol might deal with the problem described in episode #5. Create your own ending to that episode. Illustrate and narrate it below.

_____

_____

_____

✓ *Exercise #32*
*Make up a short situation that ends with ¡**Qué vergüenza!** Illustrate and narrate your original story below.*

primera lectura:
el mono malcriado

Hay una familia. En la familia hay un papá, una mamá, un muchacho que se llama Carlitos y un mono. El mono se llama Manolo. Manolo es muy malcriado. El lunes, el papá de Carlitos pasa la aspiradora en la sala de la casa. Manolo desenchufa la aspiradora y se ríe (je-je). Entonces el papá pasa la aspiradora en el dormitorio de Carlitos pero Manolo desenchufa la aspiradora otra vez y se ríe otra vez (je-je). Entonces el papá pasa la aspiradora en su oficina pero Manolo desenchufa la aspiradora por tercera vez. El papá dice «Manolo es un mono malcriado.»

El martes, a las cuatro de la mañana, el papá, la mamá, y Carlitos duermen. Pero Manolo no duerme. Manolo prende la radio con mucho volumen. ¡Qué ruido! Ahora la familia de Carlitos no duerme. Manolo se ríe pero la familia de Carlitos no se ríe. La mamá de Carlitos dice «Manolo es un mono muy malcriado.»

El miércoles, el teléfono suena. Manolo abre la puerta del refrigerador, pone el teléfono en el refrigerador y cierra la puerta. El teléfono todavía suena. El papá busca el teléfono. La mamá busca el teléfono. Por fin el papá abre el refrigerador. ¡Allí está el teléfono! Pero ahora el teléfono no suena. ¡Qué problema! Los padres de Carlitos dicen «Manolo es un mono bastante malcriado.»

El jueves, los padres de Carlitos abren la puerta del garaje. Ponen a Manolo en el garaje y cierran la puerta. ¡Pobre Manolo! Ahora Manolo no se ríe. Pero Manolo es un mono muy inteligente. Hay una lámpara en el garaje. Manolo prende y apaga la lámpara. Prende y apaga la lámpara otra vez en la forma de un S.O.S. Llega la policía a la casa de Carlitos. **¡Ay, qué malcriado es ese mono!**

Exercise #33

The story on page 24 contains many words which you have not seen before. Some of the new words look almost the same in Spanish as they do in English. These words are called cognates. List below as many new cognates as you can find in the story.

_____   _____   _____

_____   _____   _____

_____   _____   _____

Exercise #34

Some of the new words in the story "el mono malcriado" are NOT cognates, and you have to figure them out from context. The three words listed below are important new vocabulary in the story "el mono malcriado." Find all of these words in the story and circle them. Then figure out what they mean, WITHOUT using a dictionary, and write the English definition for each word in the space provided below.

1. se ríe   2. dice   3. pone

Exercise #35

When you read a new story in Spanish, you will find some new words that are hard to figure out without a dictionary. It is NOT necessary to understand every word in order to understand the story. Read the story "el mono malcriado" again and find at least four new words for which you do not know the English meaning.

_____   _____

_____   _____

_____   _____

Are there some words in your list above for which you NEED to know the English meaning in order to understand the story? Circle those words, look them up in the dictionary, and write the English meaning next to them.

✓ *Exercise #36*
Read "el mono malcriado" again. Then answer the following questions.

1. ¿Qué hay en la familia?

2. ¿Cómo se llama el muchacho?

3. ¿Cómo es Manolo?

4. ¿Qué hace el papá el lunes?

5. ¿Cuál es el problema el lunes?

6. ¿Por qué dice la mamá «Manolo es un mono muy malcriado.» ?

7. ¿Dónde está el teléfono?

8. ¿Por qué ponen los padres a Manolo en el garaje?

9. ¿Qué hace Manolo en el garaje?

✓ *Exercise #37*
Pick your favorite day (Monday, Tuesday, Wednesday or Thursday) from the story "el mono malcriado" and illustrate it below.

✓ *Exercise #38*

Imagine what happens when the police arrive at Carlitos' house. Illustrate and narrate a brief conclusion for "el mono malcriado."

_____

_____

_____

_____

_____

_____

_____

_____

27

episodio #6

Exercise #39
Practice telling episode #6. Use all of the words from the list below.

trota	el sombrero	la ropa
llora	llama por teléfono	se pone
explica	preferido/preferida	¡Qué engañoso!
	(está) desesperado/desesperada	

Exercise #40
The sentences below are false. Change each sentence to make it true.

1. Gabi llama por teléfono a Marisol.

2. Marisol está muy contenta cuando llama a Gabi.

3. Marisol le explica la solución a Gabi por teléfono.

4. Gabi camina despacio a la casa de Marisol.

5. Marisol se ríe en el teléfono.

6. Marisol tiene una idea.

Exercise #41
Answer the following questions about episode #6.

1. ¿Qué día es?

2. ¿Dónde está Marisol?

3. ¿Dónde está Gabi?

4. ¿Cómo comunica Marisol con Gabi?

5. ¿Cómo está Marisol?

29

✔ *Exercise #42*

Review all of the vocabulary words which you learned in episodes #1-6. Then select the best word to complete each sentence below.

1.   Hay un muchacho biencriado con la _____ elegante.

2.   Hoy es martes. Mañana es _____.

3.   En una emergencia, mamá _____ _____

     _____ a la policía.

4.   Pablo tiene hambre y _____ seis enchiladas.

5.   El lunes, Evita duerme. El martes, Evita duerme _____

     _____.

6.   El lunes, hay un _____ de sorpresa en la escuela.

7.   El pobre insecto _____ _____ al automóvil grande.

✔ *Exercise #43*

Use each of the following vocabulary words in an original sentence.
1.   sucio

2.   cierra

3.   trota

4.   se pone

5.   suena

✓ *Exercise #44*
Use at least two words from episode #5 and two words from episode #6 to create an original mini-story. Illustrate and narrate your story below.

episodio #7

✓ *Exercise #45*
Practice telling episode #7. Use all of the words from the list below.

camina	el pupitre	el sábado
la clase	toma	tiene
se sienta	engaña	¡Qué travieso!

✓ *Exercise #46*
The sentences below are false. Change each sentence to make it true.

1. Gabi camina a la casa de Marisol.

2. Gabi llora en el pupitre de Marisol.

3. Gabi come el examen de Marisol.

4. El profesor engaña a Gabi.

5. Gabi come a otro estudiante.

6. El otro estudiante duerme mucho.

✓ *Exercise #47*
Answer the following questions about episode #7.

1. ¿A dónde va Gabi?

2. ¿Cómo llega Gabi a la escuela de Marisol?

3. ¿Dónde se sienta Gabi?

4. ¿Qué come Gabi?

5. ¿Quién es traviesa?

✓ **Exercise #48**
Your teacher will describe a silly scene to you. Illustrate the scene below. Include as many details as you can.

✓ **Exercise #49**
Write at least three Spanish sentences describing the picture you drew in Exercise #48 above.

_____

_____

_____

_____

_____

_____

Exercise #50

Study the illustrations for a different version of episode #7. Narrate this new story below.

_____

_____

_____

_____

_____

_____

_____

_____

episodio #8

✓ *Exercise #51*

Practice telling episode #8. Use all of the words from the list below.

el domingo	la vecindad	se abren
el control remoto	el garaje/los garajes	se cierran
sale	se prenden	¡Qué curioso!
	se apagan	

✓ *Exercise #52*

The sentences below are false. Change each sentence to make it true.

1. Es sábado.

2. Gabi come el televisor.

3. Gabi trota por la casa.

4. Las puertas de los garajes se prenden y se apagan.

✓ *Exercise #53*

Answer the following questions about episode #8.

1. ¿Qué día es?

2. ¿Qué come Gabi?

3. ¿A dónde va Gabi?

4. ¿Qué pasa con las puertas de los garajes?

5. ¿Por qué se apagan y se prenden las televisiones de la vecindad?

✓ *Exercise #54*
Choose your favorite episode from #5, #6, #7 or #8 and retell it in the space provided below. Try to add a few extra details that were not given in the original story.

episodio # _____

_____

_____

_____

_____

_____

_____

_____

_____

_____

_____

_____

_____

_____

_____

_____

_____

_____

✓ *Exercise #55*
Create a sequel for episode #8. The first picture of the sequel has been provided for you. Illustrate and narrate your original sequel below.

_____

_____

_____

_____

_____

_____

_____

_____

_____

episodio #9

✓ *Exercise #56*
Practice telling episode #9. Use all of the words from the list below.

luce	recita	el poema
el juez/los jueces	gana	preparan
la competencia de belleza	el premio	¡Qué talento!

✓ *Exercise #57*
Complete the following sentences with the word or words which make the sentence true.

1. Gabi entra en la _____

_____ _____ .

2. Los amigos de Gabi la _____ .

3. Gabi _____ la competencia.

4. Los _____ le dan a Gabi un _____
grande.

✓ *Exercise #58*
Answer the following questions about episode #9.

1. ¿Qué tipo de competencia hay?

2. ¿Qué hacen los amigos de Gabi?

3. ¿Qué hace Gabi en la competencia?

4. ¿Qué le dan los jueces a Gabi?

5. En tu opinión, ¿cuál es el premio que gana Gabi?

✓ **Exercise #59**

Look at the two similar pictures below. Describe how picture #2 differs from picture #1.

1. *La gorila #2 tiene la nariz grande.*

2. _____

3. _____

4. _____

5. _____

6. _____

✓ *Exercise #60*
*Make up a short situation that ends with ¡**Qué travieso!**, ¡**Qué talento!**, or*
*¡**Qué curioso**! Illustrate and narrate your original story below.*

_____

_____

_____

_____

_____

_____

_____

_____

episodio #10

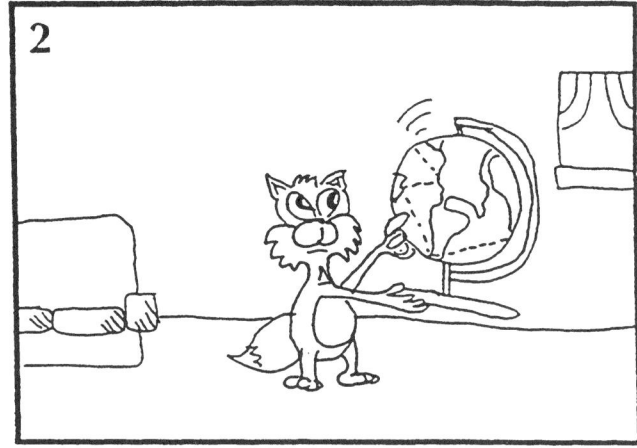

✓ *Exercise #61*
Practice telling episode #10. Use all of the words from the list below.

el barco de vela	el viaje	por fin
hace planes	practica	se despide
hace las maletas	(no) tiene talento	¡Buen viaje!
	(está) preparado/preparada	

✓ *Exercise #62*
You will hear four questions about episode #10. After you hear each question, read the three possible answers and circle the best answer.

1. a. Es un barco de vela.

    b. Gabi gana el premio.

    c. El juez gana el premio.

2. a. Gabi pone la ropa en las maletas.

    b. Gabi se pone la ropa.

    c. Hay dos maletas.

3. a. Gabi hace las maletas.

    b. Gabi se despide de sus amigos.

    c. Gabi no tiene talento con los barcos.

4. a. Gabi se despide de sus amigos.

    b. Gabi practica y practica.

    c. Gabi recita un poema original.

✓ *Exercise #63*
Answer the following questions about episode #10 using complete sentences.

1. ¿Qué premio gana Gabi?

2. ¿Qué planes hace Gabi?

3. ¿Cómo se prepara Gabi para su viaje?

4. ¿Por qué practica Gabi con el barco de vela?

45

✓ *Exercise #64*
Choose any three pictures from episode #10, and narrate them below. Add one extra detail, not given in the original story, to each of your narrations.

<u>Picture#</u>   <u>Narration</u>

_____   _____

               _____

               _____

               _____

_____   _____

               _____

               _____

               _____

_____   _____

               _____

               _____

               _____

✓ *Exercise #65*
*The new mini-story below is incomplete. It has only a middle. Read the
middle part of the story and provide a logical beginning and ending.*

●

_____

_____

_____

_____

_____

●

Paco se pone el suéter. El suéter es muy grande. ¡Qué

sorpresa! Hay un billete de lotería en el suéter.

_____

_____

_____

_____

●

_____

_____

segunda lectura:
el amigo invisible

Hay una muchacha que se llama Nela. Nela tiene un amigo especial. Es especial porque es invisible. Es invisible a todos menos Nela. Es un buen amigo. Un día Nela está en la escuela. Está en la clase de matemáticas. El profesor dice «Hay un examen de sorpresa.» ¡Qué horror! Nela está desesperada porque ella no tiene mucho talento con las matemáticas y no está preparada para el examen. De repente, el amigo invisible de Nela entra en la clase. Se sienta en la silla del profesor. Los exámenes están en el escritorio del profesor. El amigo invisible toma los exámenes y pone los exámenes en el sombrero del profesor. El profesor busca los exámenes. Busca los exámenes en el escritorio pero no están allí. Busca los exámanes debajo de su escritorio pero no están allí. El profesor no encuentra los exámenes. El amigo invisible se ríe. Después de la clase Nela le dice «gracias» a su amigo invisible.

Entonces Nela y su amigo invisible regresan a casa. La mamá de Nela le dice «Nela, ¡practica el piano!» Nela practica pero no toca el piano bien. Nela no tiene mucho talento músico. Entonces el amigo invisible toca el piano. Toca muy bien. La mamá de Nela le dice «Nela, la música es muy bonita.» Nela le dice «gracias» a su amigo invisible.

El próximo día, hay una competencia literaria en la escuela. Nela no está preparada. Nela tiene parte de un poema pero es un poema muy malo y no está completo. Nela no tiene mucho talento literario. Nela busca a su amigo invisible. Pero el amigo no está. ¡El amigo todavía está en casa! ¡Todavía duerme! ¡Caramba! Pobre Nela. Nela recita su poema pero no gana el primer premio. No gana el segundo premio. No gana el tercer premio. Nela no gana nada. **¡Qué vergüenza!**

✓ Exercise #66

The story on page 48 contains many words which you have not seen before. Some of the new words look almost the same in Spanish as they do in English. These words are called cognates. List below as many new cognates as you can find in the story.

_____   _____   _____

_____   _____   _____

_____   _____   _____

✓ Exercise #67

Some of the new words in the story "el amigo invisible" are NOT cognates, and you have to figure them out from context. The three words listed below are important new vocabulary in the story "el amigo invisible." Find all of these words in the story and circle them. Then figure out what they mean, WITHOUT using a dictionary, and write the English definition for each word in the space provided below.

1. toca   2. el escritorio   3. nada

✓ Exercise #68

When you read a new story in Spanish, you will find some new words that are hard to figure out without a dictionary. It is NOT necessary to understand every word in order to understand the story. Read the story "el amigo invisible" again and find at least four new words for which you do not know the English meaning.

_____   _____

_____   _____

_____   _____

Are there some words in your list above for which you NEED to know the English meaning in order to understand the story? Circle those words, look them up in the dictionary, and write the English meaning next to them.

✓ *Exercise #69*
Read "el amigo invisible" again. Then answer the following questions.

1. ¿Por qué es especial el amigo de Nela?

2. ¿Qué tipo de examen tiene el profesor?

3. ¿Qué hace el amigo de Nela con los exámenes?

4. ¿Qué tipo de talento tiene el amigo de Nela?

5. ¿Cómo es el poema de Nela?

6. ¿Dónde está el amigo de Nela cuando Nela recita su poema?

7. ¿Qué gana Nela?

✓ *Exercise #70*
Nela's friend does two favors for Nela. Illustrate each of the favors below.

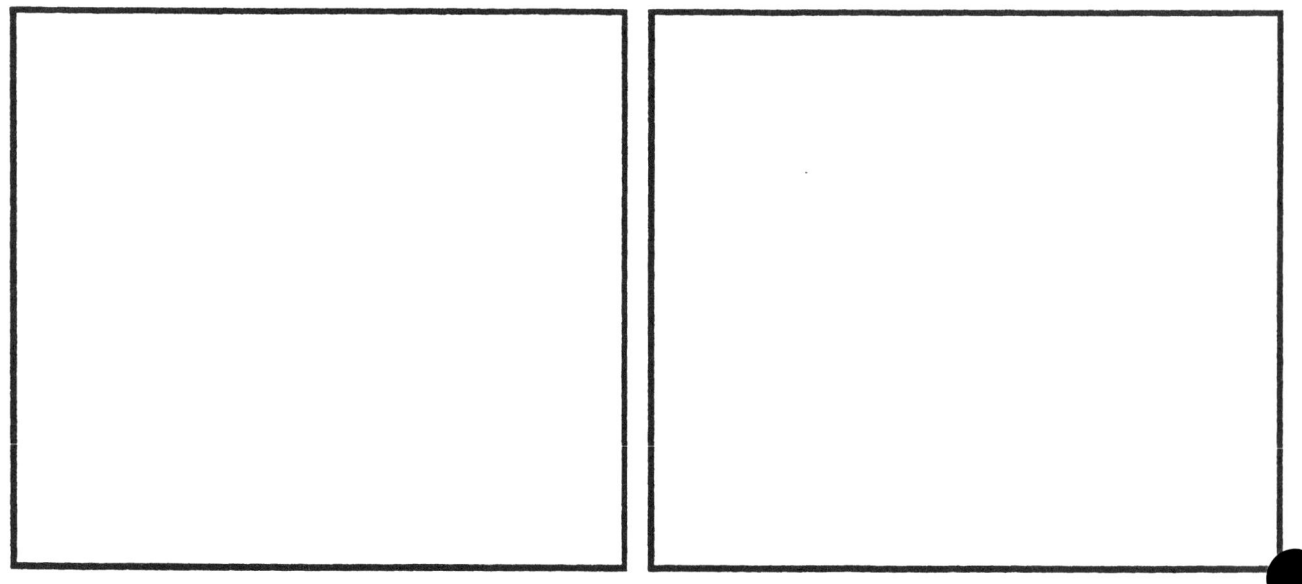

Exercise #71

During their friendship, Nela's invisible friend does many favors for her. The story, "el amigo invisible," only describes two of these favors. Create a story about another favor the invisible friend does for Nela. Illustrate and narrate your original story below.

_____

_____

_____

_____

_____

_____

_____

episodio #11

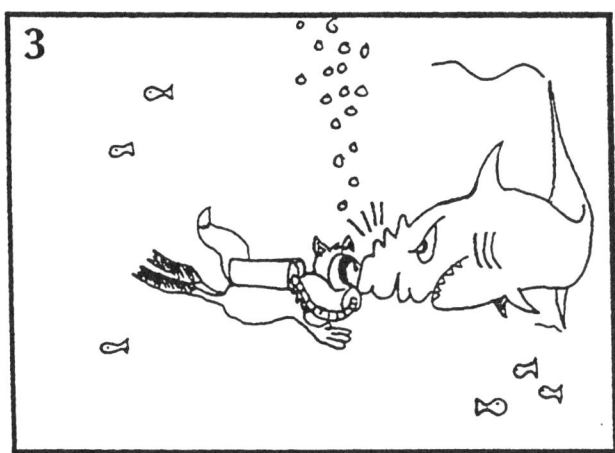

✓ *Exercise #72*
Practice telling episode #11. Use all of the words from the list below.

navega	se choca (con)	tiene (mucho) miedo
el mar	el tiburón	se hunde
bucea	muerde	¡Socorro!

✓ *Exercise #73*
The sentences below are false. Change each sentence to make it true.

1. Gabi trota por el mar en su barco de vela.

2. Un día, el tiburón bucea.

3. En el mar, Gabi se choca con un elefante.

4. Gabi tiene hambre.

5. El tiburón tiene miedo.

6. Gabi muerde la nariz del tiburón.

7. El tiburón dice «¡Socorro!»

✓ **Exercise #74**
Retell episode #11 in your own words.

_____

_____

_____

_____

_____

_____

_____

_____

_____

_____

_____

_____

_____

_____

_____

_____

_____

✓ *Exercise #75*
Your teacher will describe a scene to you. Illustrate that scene below.
Include as many details as you can.

✓ *Exercise #76*
Write at least three Spanish sentences describing the scene you drew above
in Exercise #75.

_____

_____

_____

_____

_____

_____

✓ ***Exercise #77: What's Missing? (Part A)***
Look at the first and last pictures of the new story below. Complete the story with some original pictures.

Exercise #78: What's Missing? (Part B)
Write out the story which you just illustrated.

episodio #12

✓ *Exercise #79*
Practice telling episode #12. Use all of the words from the list below.

de repente	sube	la isla
el avión	vuela	¡Qué alivio!
estornuda	se cae	¡Qué suerte!

✓ *Exercise #80*
Answer the following questions about episode #12.

1. ¿Por qué sube en el aire Gabi?

2. ¿Cómo sale Gabi del mar?

3. ¿Qué pasa cuando Gabi se pega al avión?

4. ¿Cómo está Gabi cuando ella vuela con el avión?

5. ¿Qué pasa cuando Gabi estornuda otra vez?

✓ *Exercise #81*
There are some details which could be added to the story in episode #12 to make it more complete. Use your imagination to answer the following questions.

1. ¿En cuál océano está Gabi?

2. ¿Cómo es el avión?

3. ¿A dónde vuela el avión?

4. ¿A cuál isla llega Gabi?

✓ *Exercise #82*
Choose any three pictures from episode #12, and narrate them below. Add one extra detail, not given in the original story, to each of your narrations.

Picture#   *Narration*

_____   _____

_____

_____

_____

_____   _____

_____

_____

_____

_____   _____

_____

_____

_____

✓ *Exercise #83*
*Make up a short situation that ends with **¡Qué alivio!** Illustrate and narrate your original story below.*

episodio #13

Exercise #84
Practice telling episode #13. Use all of the words from the list below.

(está) curioso/curiosa	**el ramo**	**se enoja**
explora	**el árbol**	**¡Dale!**
	el mono	

Exercise #85
Answer the following questions about episode #13.

1. ¿Dónde está Gabi?

2. ¿Cómo está Gabi ahora?

3. ¿Qué hace Gabi primero?

4. ¿Qué come Gabi?

5. ¿Quién duerme?

6. En tu opinión, ¿qué hay en la isla?

Exercise #86
Write three or four sentences describing the picture below.

_____

_____

_____

_____

_____

_____

_____

✓ **Exercise #87**
Your teacher will describe
three silly scenes to you.
Illustrate each of those
scenes in the boxes below.

✓ **Exercise #88**
Now describe each of the silly scenes you
drew in Exercise #87.

Exercise #89

Choose any three pictures from episode #13, and narrate them below. Add one extra detail, not given in the original story, to each of your narrations.

Picture#   Narration

_____   _____

                _____

                _____

                _____

_____   _____

                _____

                _____

                _____

_____   _____

                _____

                _____

                _____

✓ *Exercise #90: What's Missing? (Part A)*
Look at the first and last pictures of the new story below. Complete the story with some original pictures.

Exercise #91: What's Missing? (Part B)
Write out the story which you just illustrated.

episodio #14

✓ *Exercise #92*
Practice telling episode #14. Use all of the words from the list below.

encuentra	la cima	hace (mucho) calor
el rey	el volcán	¡Qué sabroso/sabrosa!
lleva	le da una patada	¡Qué horror!

✓ *Exercise #93*
The sentences below are false. Change each sentence to make it true.

1. El rey de la isla encuentra a Gabi.

2. El rey lleva la ropa elegante.

3. El rey todavía tiene hambre.

4. El rey está muy contento.

5. Gabi come al rey.

6. El rey lleva a Gabi a un barco de vela.

✓ *Exercise #94*
Answer the following questions about episode #14.

1. ¿Qué hay en la isla?

2. ¿Por qué se enoja el rey?

3. ¿A dónde lleva el rey a Gabi?

4. ¿Quién le da una patada a Gabi?

5. ¿Qué tiempo hace en el volcán?

✔ **_Exercise #95_**
Narrate the new story you see illustrated below.

_____

_____

_____

_____

_____

_____

_____

_____

_____

✓ *Exercise #96*
Make up a short situation that ends with ¡Qué sabroso! or ¡Qué horror!
Illustrate and narrate your original story below.

episodio #15

✓ *Exercise #97*
Practice telling episode #15. Use all of the words from the list below.

explota	se ríe	el esquimal
vive	va de caza	da
aplasta	invita	¡Ojo!

✓ *Exercise #98*
Answer the following questions about episode #15.

1. ¿Cómo llega Gabi a Alaska?

2. ¿Quién vive en Alaska?

3. ¿Se enoja el esquimal?

4. ¿A dónde van el esquimal y Gabi?

5. ¿Por qué es un error darle un rifle a Gabi?

✓ **Exercise #99**
Review all of the vocabulary words which you learned in episodes #12-15.
Then select the best word to complete each sentence below.

1. Javier hace una fiesta grande e _____ a todos
    sus amigos.

2. Cuando un hombre prehistórico tiene hambre, él

    _____ _____ _____ .

3. El explorador famoso _____ la montaña grande.

4. Los aviones _____ rápido en el aire.

5. En Arizona en junio, julio y agosto hace mucho _____ .

6. Los modelos _____ la ropa muy bonita.

7. Una persona de buen humor siempre _____ _____ .

✓ **Exercise #100**
Write three or four sentences describing the picture below. In each sentence,
use a new vocabulary word from episode #15.

_____

_____

_____

_____

_____

✓ *Exercise #101*
Choose your favorite episode from #12, #13, #14 or #15 and retell it in the space provided below. Try to add a few extra details that were not given in the original story.

episodio #————

tercera lectura:
Rafael y los piratas

primera parte: ¡accidente en el mar!

Hay un muchacho que se llama Rafael. Un día Rafael va de viaje en su barco de vela. Navega al centro del océano. Entonces tiene hambre. Saca su caña de pescar y pesca. Pero, hay un problema. Hay otro barco en el océano. ¡Ojo! ¡El otro barco es un barco de piratas! Rafael tiene mucho miedo.

El barco de los piratas es muy grande y los piratas navegan muy rápido al barco de Rafael. Pero el barco de Rafael es pequeño y Rafael no navega rápido. Los piratas se acercan más y más a Rafael. Por fin, el barco de los piratas se choca con el barco de Rafael. Rafael se cae en el mar. Entonces Rafael nada. Nada muy bien y muy rápido y llega a una isla.

Al llegar a la isla, Rafael explora la isla. En la isla hay muchas rocas y una montaña. En la cima de la montaña hay un árbol. No hay nada más en la isla. No hay flores. No hay animales. Sólo hay rocas, una montaña y un árbol. Hace mucho calor en la isla porque hace mucho sol. Rafael sube la montaña y se sienta debajo del árbol. No está muy contento. Está desilusionado.

segunda parte: ¡tesoro!

De repente, los piratas llegan a la isla. Los piratas tienen rifles. ¡Ojo! Pero, los piratas no buscan a Rafael. No buscan nada. Los piratas tienen un tesoro grande. El tesoro es muchas joyas: diamantes, rubís, esmeraldas y zafiros. Los piratas ponen el tesoro debajo de una roca grande y salen. Rafael llama a los piratas «¡Socorro!» Pero los piratas le dicen «Adiós, señor» a Rafael y salen en su barco.

Los piratas navegan en el mar. Pero de repente, muchos tiburones muy grandes llegan. Los tiburones tienen hambre. Se chocan con el barco de los piratas. Los piratas se caen en el mar. Ahora los piratas tienen miedo porque no nadan muy bien.

Entretanto, Rafael sale de la cima de la montaña. Mueve la roca grande y toma el tesoro. Ahora Rafael tiene muchas joyas pero todavía tiene un problema. Rafael tiene hambre y no hay nada de comer.

Pero, de repente, llega un barco muy grande a la isla. No es un barco de vela. No es un barco de piratas. Es un yate elegante. Y, ¡qué sorpresa, el capitán del yate es el amigo de Rafael! Rafael sube al yate con el tesoro de los piratas y el yate sale de la isla. En el mar el yate pasa los piratas que están en el agua. Los piratas llaman a Rafael, «¡Socorro!»

¿Qué les dice Rafael a los piratas?

✔ *Exercise #102*

The story on pages 76-77 contains many words which you have not seen before. Some of the new words look almost the same in Spanish as they do in English. These words are called cognates. List below as many new cognates as you can find in "Rafael y los piratas."

_____   _____   _____

_____   _____   _____

_____   _____   _____

✔ *Exercise #103*

Some of the new words in the story "Rafael y los piratas" are NOT cognates, and you have to figure them out from context. The three words listed below are important new vocabulary in the story "Rafael y los piratas." Find all of these words in the story and circle them. Then figure out what they mean, WITHOUT using a dictionary, and write the English definition for each word in the space provided below.

   1. se acercan   2. nada   3. el tesoro

✔ *Exercise #104*

When you read a new story in Spanish, you will find some new words that are hard to figure out without a dictionary. It is NOT necessary to understand every word in order to understand the story. Read the story again and find at least four new words for which you do not know the English meaning. List those words below.

_____   _____

_____   _____

_____   _____

_____   _____

Are there some words in your list above for which you NEED to know the English meaning in order to understand the story? Circle those words, look them up in the dictionary, and write the English meaning next to them.

Exercise #105
Read "Rafael y los piratas" again. Then answer the following questions.

1. ¿Qué tipo de barco tiene Rafael?

2. ¿De quién es el otro barco?

3. ¿Cómo es el barco de Rafael?

4. ¿Cómo es el otro barco?

5. ¿Por qué se cae en el mar Rafael?

6. ¿Cómo es la isla?

7. ¿Dónde se sienta Rafael?

8. ¿Qué buscan los piratas en la isla?

Exercise #106
Create a conclusion for "Rafael y los piratas." Narrate it below.

_____

_____

_____

_____

_____

_____

_____

_____

episodio #16

✓ *Exercise #107*
Practice telling episode #16. Use all of the words from the list below.

van de pesca	la caña de pescar	el lago
hace (mucho) frío	corta	salva
el abrigo	el hielo	¡Qué desgracia!

✓ *Exercise #108*
The sentences below are false. Change each sentence to make it true.

1. Hace mucho calor en Alaska.

2. El esquimal le da un sombrero a Gabi.

3. Gabi y el esquimal van de caza.

4. Gabi corta un triángulo en el hielo.

5. Cuando Gabi se cae en el lago, Gabi se ríe.

6. Gabi le da al esquimal una caña de pescar.

7. Gabi salva al esquimal.

✓ *Exercise #109*
Answer the following questions about episode #16.

1. ¿Por qué se pone un abrigo Gabi?

2. ¿A dónde caminan el esquimal Gabi?

3. ¿Qué le da el esquimal a Gabi?

4. ¿Cuál es el problema en el lago?

5. ¿Cuál es la solución?

81

✓ *Exercise #110*
Look at the two similar pictures below. Describe how picture #2 differs from picture #1.

1. _____

2. _____

3. _____

4. _____

5. _____

6. _____

7. _____

Exercise #111
Make up a short situation that ends with **¡Qué desgracia!** *Illustrate and narrate your original story below.*

episodio #17

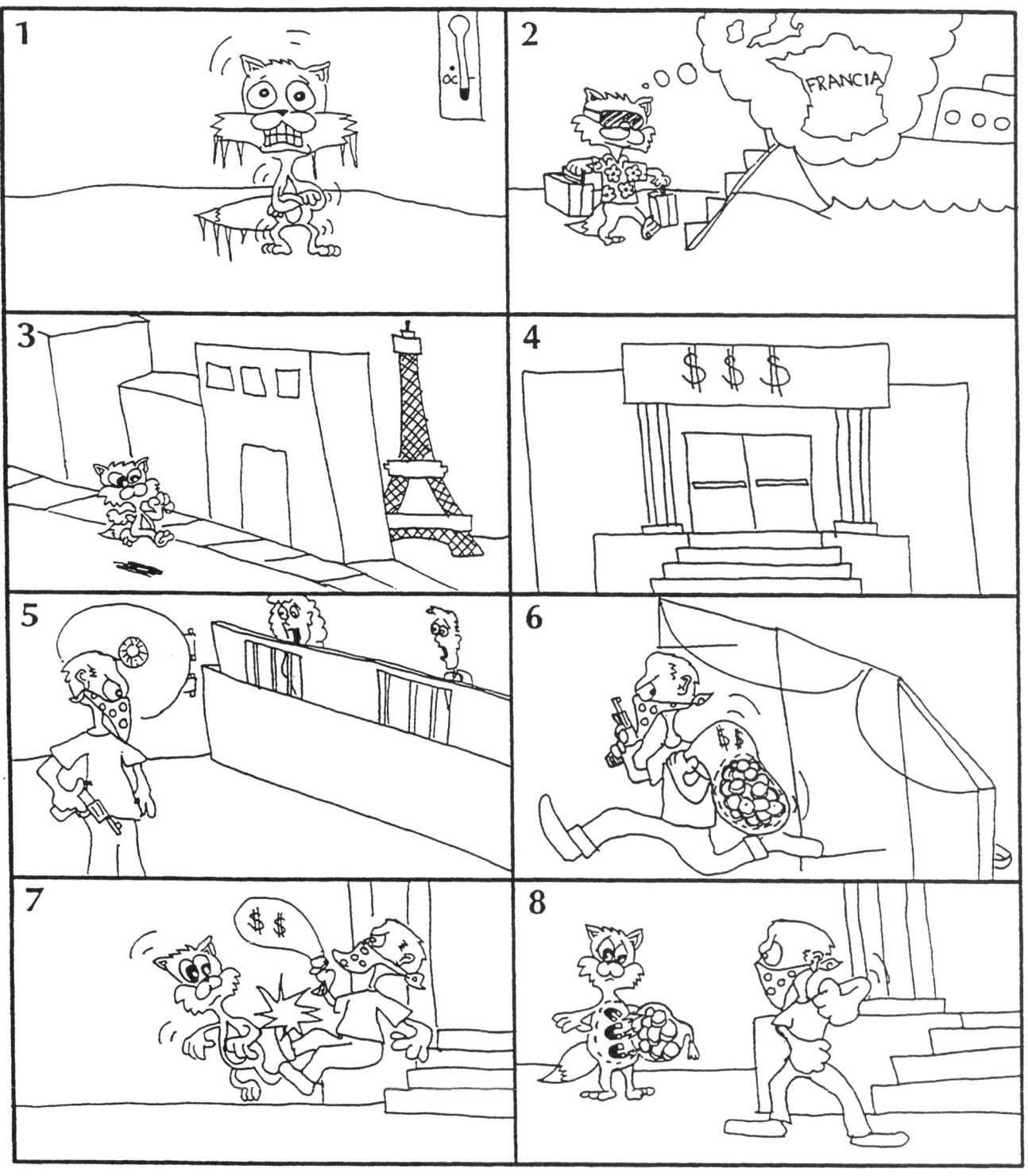

✓ *Exercise #112*
Practice telling episode #17. Use all of the words from the list below.

va de vacaciones	el ladrón	resulta una lucha
la calle	roba	las monedas
el banco	la lucha	¡Disculpe!

✓ *Exercise #113*
You will hear six questions about episode #17. After you hear each question, read the three possible answers and circle the best answer.

1. a. Está en Alaska.
    b. Está en las calles de París.
    c. Está en el banco.

2. a. Hace demasiado frío en Alaska.
    b. Hay un banco en Europa.
    c. Gabi va de vacaciones a Europa.

3. a. El ladrón roba las monedas.
    b. Hay un banco.
    c. Gabi y el ladrón se chocan.

4. a. Se chocan cuando Gabi entra en el banco.
    b. Se chocan cuando el ladrón sale del banco.
    c. Se chocan cuando Gabi sale del banco.

5. a. Se pegan cuando el ladrón sale rápido del banco.
    b. Se pegan al estómago de Gabi.
    c. Se pegan porque Gabi todavía tiene los imanes en el estómago.

6. a. Porque ahora Gabi tiene las monedas.
    b. Porque hay una lucha.
    c. Porque el ladrón sale del banco.

✓ *Exercise #114*
Answer the following questions about episode #17.

1. ¿Por qué sale Gabi de Alaska?

2. ¿A dónde va Gabi?

3. ¿Por dónde trota Gabi?

4. ¿Quién está en el banco?

5. ¿Por qué se pega Gabi a las monedas?

✓ *Exercise #115*
Retell episode #17 in your own words. CHANGE three details.

_____

_____

_____

_____

_____

_____

_____

_____

_____

_____

_____

_____

✓ Exercise #116

Below is a new story with a problem. The middle is missing. Read the beginning and the ending of this story. Then fill in the middle part to logically complete the story.

Un día, Gabi está en un banco. Entra un ladrón. ¡Ay, qué horror!

_____

_____

_____

_____

_____

_____

_____

_____

_____

_____

_____

_____

_____

Resulta que la policía le da a Gabi un premio y le dice «Muchas gracias.»

episodio #18

Exercise #117
Practice telling episode #18. Use all of the words from the list below.

se quita	la policía	(está) alarmado/alarmada
el zapato	captura	¡Bien se lo merece!
pega	el dolor de cabeza	

Exercise #118
The sentences below are false. Change each sentence to make it true.

1. El despertador suena en el estómago del ladrón.

2. El ladrón está muy calmo.

3. El ladrón se quita el suéter.

4. El ladrón se despide de Gabi con el zapato.

5. Llega Superhombre.

6. La policía captura a Gabi.

Exercise #119
Answer the following questions about episode #18.

1. ¿Qué suena?

2. ¿Cuál es la reacción del ladrón?

3. ¿Quién llega?

4. ¿Quién captura al ladrón?

5. ¿Cómo está Gabi al final del episodio?

✓ *Exercise #120: What's Missing? (Part A)*
Look at the first and last pictures of the new story below. Complete the story with some original pictures.

Exercise #121: What's Missing? (Part B)
Write out the story which you just illustrated.

episodio #19

✓ *Exercise #122*
Practice telling episode #19. Use all of the words from the list below.

la prensa	el periodista	la amnesia
la fotógrafa	entrevista	nada
saca una foto	pregunta	¡No faltaba más!
	recuerda	

✓ *Exercise #123*
The sentences below are false. Change each sentence to make it true.

1. La prensa sale del banco.

2. La fotógrafa entrevista a Gabi.

3. Gabi recuerda su nombre.

4. Gabi tiene dolor de estómago.

5. El periodista tiene amnesia.

✓ *Exercise #124*
Answer the following questions about episode #19.

1. ¿Quién llega al banco?

2. ¿A quién le saca fotos la fotógrafa?

3. ¿Qué le pregunta el periodista a Gabi?

4. ¿Recuerda Gabi cómo se llama?

5. ¿Por qué no recuerda nada Gabi?

✓ *Exercise #125*
Choose your favorite episode from #16, #17, #18 or #19 and retell it in the space provided below. Try to add a few extra details that were not given in the original story.

episodio # _____

_____

_____

_____

_____

_____

_____

_____

_____

_____

_____

_____

_____

_____

_____

_____

_____

✓ *Exercise #126*
Use at least one word from each vocabulary list for episodes #16-19 to create a new mini-story. Illustrate and narrate your original story below.

episodio #20

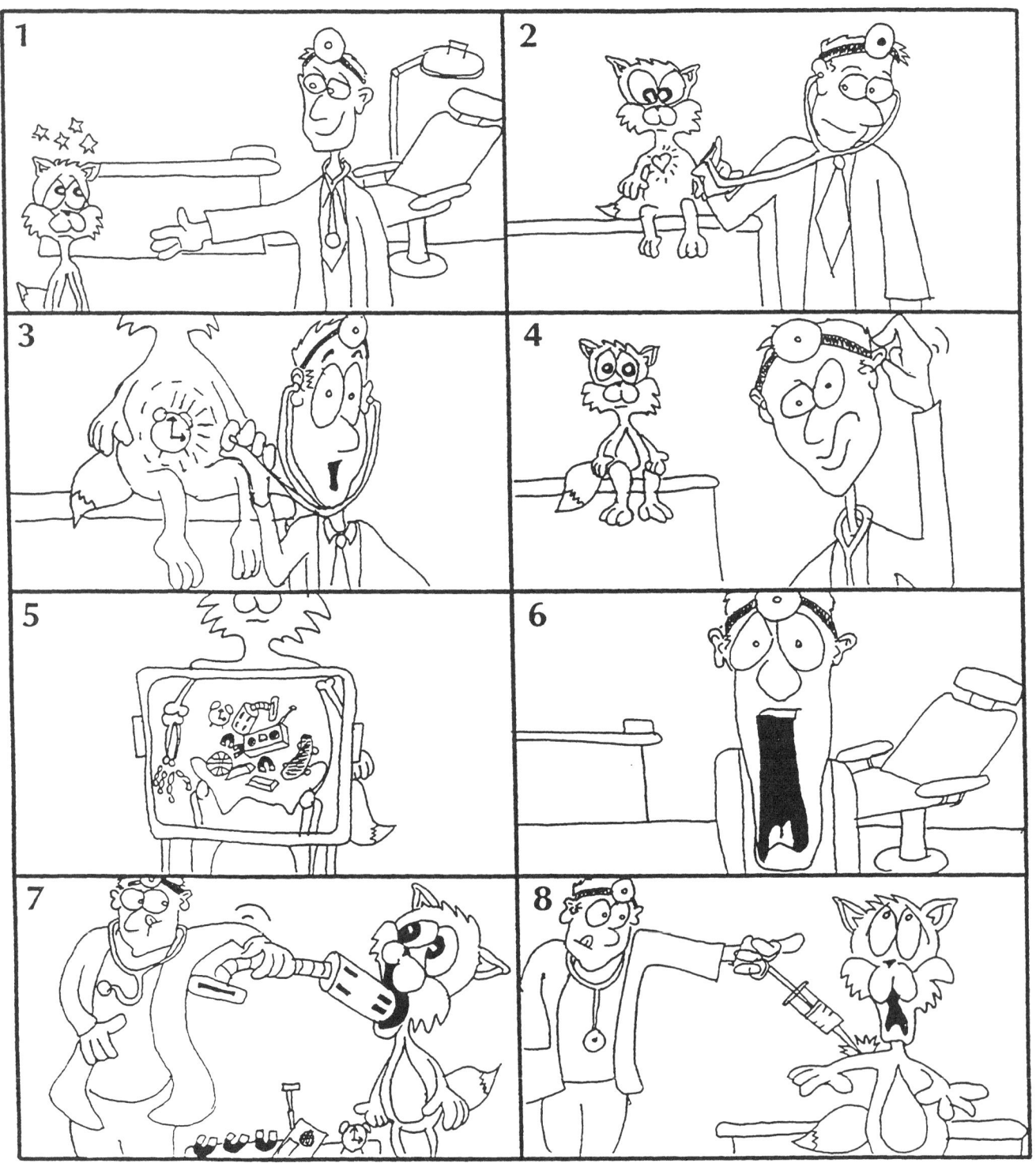

Exercise #127
Practice telling episode #20. Use all of the words from the list below.

saca	saca un rayo-equis	la inyección
escucha	(está) sorprendido/sorprendida	¡Qué extraño!
el corazón	el médico/la médica	¡Qué dolor!

Exercise #128
Complete the following sentences with the word or words which make the sentence true.

1. El médico _____ el corazón de Gabi.

2. El _____ en el estómago de Gabi hace un tic-toc.

3. El médico saca un _____ - _____.

4. El médico ve los _____, el_____,

    y la_____ en el estómago de Gabi.

5. El médico está bastante _____.

6. El médico _____ todo del estómago de Gabi.

Exercise #129
Answer the following questions about episode #20.

1. ¿A dónde va Gabi?

2. ¿Qué hace el médico?

3. ¿Qué hay en el estómago de Gabi?

4. ¿Cómo está el médico cuando examina el rayo-equis?

97

✓ *Exercise #130*

Choose any three pictures from episode #20, and narrate them below. Add one extra detail, not given in the original story, to each of your narrations.

<u>Picture#</u>   <u>Narration</u>

_____   _____

                   _____

                   _____

                   _____

_____   _____

                   _____

                   _____

                   _____

_____   _____

                   _____

                   _____

                   _____

Exercise #131

Create a short story which ends with the expression ¡Qué extraño! Use the picture provided as the starting point of your story. Illustrate and narrate your story below.

1	2
3	4

_____

_____

_____

_____

_____

_____

_____

_____

cuarta lectura:
Sabrina la aplastadora

Hay una elefante que se llama Sabrina. Sabrina vive con la familia Marisma. Todos están contentos. Un día Sabrina recuerda que es el cumpleaños de su mamá, pero no recuerda dónde vive su mamá. Sabrina tiene mucho pánico, porque por lo general los elefantes recuerdan todo. Entonces Sabrina está desesperada y sale de la casa de la familia Marisma. Sabrina busca a su madre.

Sabrina camina por la vecindad. Busca y busca a su madre. Sabrina ve un carro. Es el carro del Sr. González. Sabrina busca a su madre en el carro. Pero, ¡ojo! Sabrina es grande, y el carro es pequeño. Resulta que su mamá no está en el carro, y por accidente Sabrina aplasta el carro. ¡Caray! Sabrina tiene miedo y trota rápido. Sale el Sr. González y ve el carro aplastado. El Sr. González se enoja mucho. El Sr. González saca su red de elefantes* y va de caza. Busca a Sabrina. ¡Dale, Sabrina, dale!

Ahora Sabrina tiene hambre, pero no tiene monedas. Sabrina ve un banco en la calle. Entra en el banco, pero, ¡ojo! Sabrina es grande y la puerta es pequeña, y por accidente Sabrina aplasta la puerta del banco. ¡Caray! Sabrina tiene miedo y trota rápido. El banquero se enoja mucho. Saca su red de elefantes y va de caza. Busca a Sabrina. ¡Dale, Sabrina, dale!

Más tarde, hace mucho frío. Mucho hielo forma en la nariz de Sabrina. ¡Pobre Sabrina! Sabrina ve un abrigo en la casa de la Sra. Mateus. Sabrina saca el abrigo y se pone el abrigo. Pero, ¡ojo! El abrigo es pequeño y Sabrina es grande. ¡Caray! Sabrina se quita el abrigo, pero ahora el abrigo es muy grande y feo. Sabrina tiene miedo y trota rápido. Por accidente, Sabrina aplasta las flores de la

Sra. Mateus. La Sra. Mateus se enoja. Saca su red de elefantes y va de caza. Busca a Sabrina. ¡Dale, Sabrina, dale!

Ahora, todo el mundo está alarmado. La prensa entrevista al Sr. González, al banquero, y a la Sra. Mateus. Llega la policía y busca a Sabrina también.

Sabrina trota rápido. Pero está cansada. Por eso, se sienta en una silla en el parque. Pero, ¡ojo! Por accidente, Sabrina aplasta la silla. Sabrina llora y llora. Llega la policía. Sabrina tiene pánico. Un policía captura a Sabrina. Un fotógrafo le saca una foto a Sabrina en el parque. Sabrina va a la prisión. ¡Pobre Sabrina!

El próximo día, Sabrina está en la prisión. Está muy triste, pero hay una sorpresa. Llega la mamá de Sabrina. La mamá de Sabrina tiene la foto de Sabrina en el parque. La mamá salva a Sabrina. ¡Están muy contentas! Celebran el cumpleaños de la mamá de Sabrina en la casa de la familia Marisma. Hay música y pastel de cumpleaños para la mamá de Sabrina. Pero, ¡ojo! Por accidente la mamá de Sabrina aplasta el pastel. Sabrina y su mamá se ríen mucho.

¡Como madre, como hija!*

---

* el red de elefantes = the elephant net

* como madre como hija = like mother, like daughter

✓ *Exercise #132*

The story on page 100 contains many words which you have not seen before. Some of the new words look almost the same in Spanish as they do in English. These words are called cognates. List below as many new cognates as you can find in "Sabrina la aplastadora."

_____   _____   _____

_____   _____   _____

_____   _____   _____

✓ *Exercise #133*

Some of the new words in the story "Sabrina la aplastadora" are NOT cognates, and you have to figure them out from context. The three words listed below are important new vocabulary in the story "Sabrina la aplastadora." Find all of these words in the story and circle them. Then figure out what they mean, WITHOUT using a dictionary, and write the English definition for each word in the space provided below.

1. el cumpleaños   2. el pastel   3. se quita

✓ *Exercise #134*

When you read a new story in Spanish, you will find some new words that are hard to figure out without a dictionary. It is NOT necessary to understand every word in order to understand the story. Read the story again and find at least four new words for which you do not know the English meaning. List those words below.

_____   _____

_____   _____

_____   _____

Are there some words in your list above for which you NEED to know the English meaning in order to understand the story? Circle those words, look them up in the dictionary, and write the English meaning next to them.

Exercise #135
Read "Sabrina la aplastadora" again. Then answer the following questions.

1. ¿Por qué sale Sabrina de la casa de la familia Marisma?

2. ¿Qué aplasta Sabrina primero?

   ¿Segundo?

   ¿Tercero?

3. ¿Qué pasa en el parque?

4. ¿Qué pasa en la prisión?

5. ¿Cómo sale Sabrina de la prisión?

6. ¿Qué pasa en la fiesta de cumpleaños?

✓ *Exercise #136*
Select four of Sabrina's encounters (either with Mr. González, the banker, Mrs. Mateus, in the park, in the jail, or at the party). Illustrate each of the four encounters below.

Exercise #137

Imagine a day in the life of Sabrina's mother. Illustrate and narrate a brief, original story below. Remember, "Like mother, like daughter!"

episodio #21

✓ Exercise #138
Practice telling episode #21. Use all of the words from the list below.

baila   el elefante   aprende
tiene (mucha) suerte   (es) famoso/famosa   ¡Qué lástima!
conoce   el ballet

✓ Exercise #139
Answer the following questions about episode #21.

1. ¿Qué busca Gabi?

2. ¿Tiene suerte Gabi?

3. ¿A quién conoce Gabi?

4. ¿Cómo es el amigo nuevo de Gabi?

5. ¿Qué hacen Gabi y Leopoldo?

6. ¿Está contenta Gabi? ¿Por qué sí o por qué no?

✓ Exercise #140
The sentences below are false. Change each sentence to make it true.

1. Gabi busca su memoria en Europa.

2. Gabi tiene suerte en Europa.

3. Gabi viaja a México.

4. En Asia, Gabi conoce a una llama que se llama Leonarda.

5. El nuevo amigo de Gabi baila flamenco.

6. Gabi y Marisol bailan por toda Asia.

107

✓ *Exercise #141*
Below is the beginning of a revision of episode #21. Change the name of the country Gabi visits and create a new ending for the story. Then illustrate the final scene of your new story in the space provided.

Gabi todavía no recuerda nada. Busca un amigo en Europa.

pero no tiene suerte. Entonces Gabi sube a un barco y viaja a

✓ *Exercise #142*

Create an original story about Leopoldo. You might choose to write about his family, his friends, his school life, his dancing career or his travels. Illustrate and narrate your original story below.

episodio #22

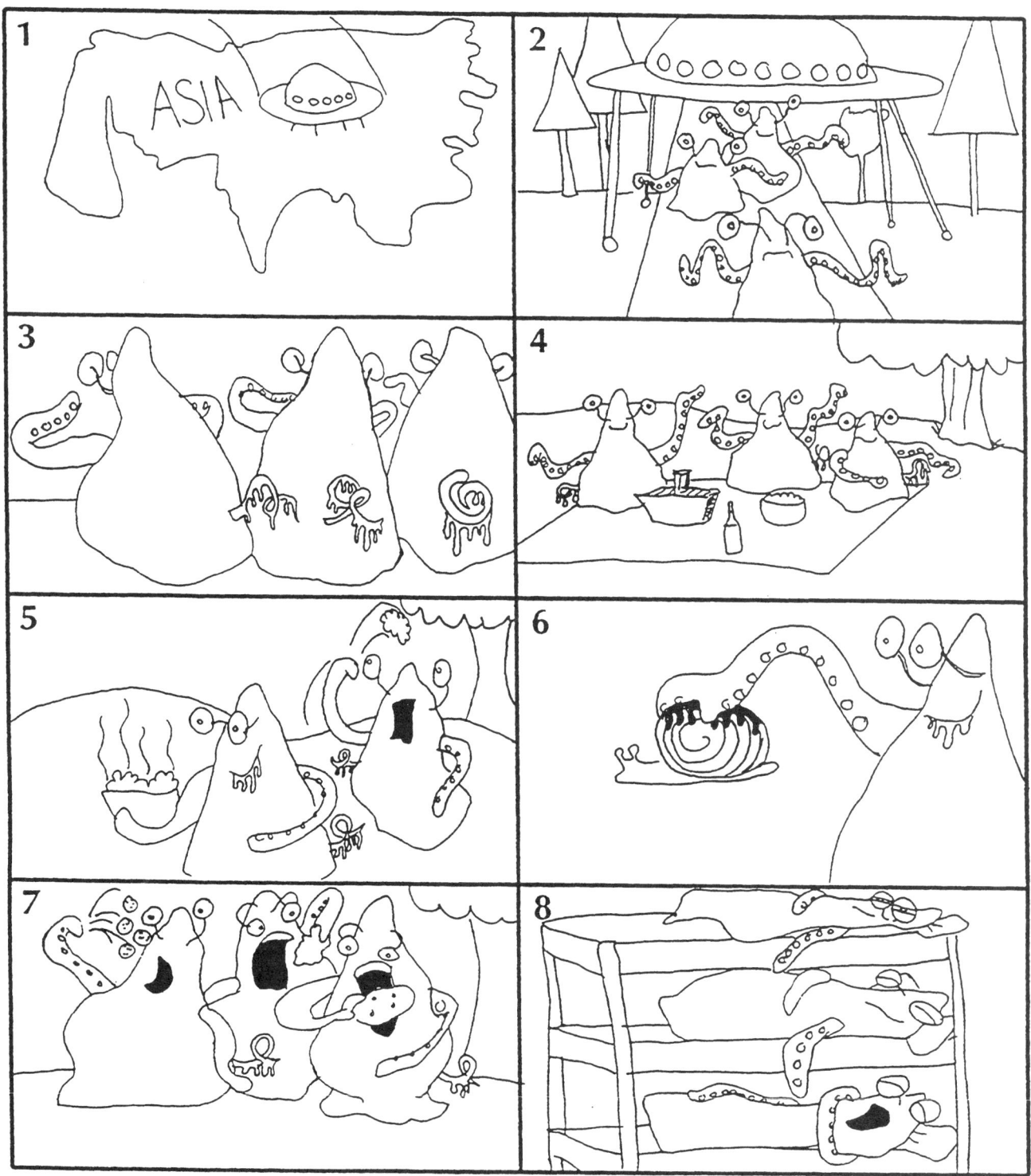

Exercise #143
Practice telling episode #22. Use all of the words from the list below.

la nave espacial	**(es) rizado/rizada**	**(están) cansados/cansadas**
los extraterrestres	**(es) viscoso/viscosa**	**la comida**
(son) feos/feas	**hacen un picnic**	**¡Qué disgusto!**
	los caracoles	

Exercise #144
Answer the following questions about episode #22.

1. ¿A dónde llega la nave espacial?

2. ¿Quiénes salen de la nave espacial?

3. ¿Qué comen los extraterrestres?

4. Después del picnic ¿cómo están los extraterrestres?

Exercise #145
The sentences below are false. Change each sentence to make it true.

1. Llega un barco espacial a Asia.

2. Salen tres serpientes.

3. Los extraterrestres hacen una barbacoa.

4. Comen hamburguesas con chocolate.

5. Los extraterrestres tienen el pelo rizado.

✓ **Exercise #146**
Your teacher will describe three silly scenes to you. Illustrate each of those scenes in the boxes below.

✓ **Exercise #147**
Now describe each of the silly scenes you drew in Exercise #146.

Exercise #148
Create a story about extraterrestrials. Illustrate and narrate your original story below.

episodio #23

Exercise #149
Practice telling episode #23. Use all of the words from the list below.

huele	se tropieza	¡Qué peligro!
no aguanta más	empuja	¡Caray!
el volumen	(no) se da cuenta	

Exercise #150
Answer the following questions about episode #23.

1. ¿Qué huele Gabi?

2. ¿Por qué entra Gabi en la nave espacial?

3. ¿Cuánto volumen tiene la música en la nave espacial?

4. ¿Cuál accidente pasa en la nave?

5. ¿Por qué no se da cuenta del accidente Gabi?

Exercise #151
The sentences below are false. Change each sentence to make it true.

1. Cuando Gabi trota por Africa, encuentra la nave espacial.

2. Gabi huele la música extraterrestre.

3. Gabi aguanta mucho y no entra en la nave.

4. Gabi duerme dentro de la nave.

5. Gabi se tropieza y se pega a los controles.

6. Cuando la nave espacial sube, Gabi tiene pánico.

115

✓ **Exercise #152: What's Missing? (Part A)**
Look at the first and last pictures of the new story below. Complete the story with some original pictures.

Exercise #153: What's Missing? (Part B)
Write out the story which you just illustrated.

episodio #24

✓ *Exercise #154*
Practice telling episode #24. Use all of the words from the list below.

se despiertan	**la cama**	**el techo**
el ruido	**descubren**	**¡Increíble!**
	flota	

✓ *Exercise #155*
Answer the following questions about episode #24.

1. ¿Por qué se despiertan los extraterrestres?

2. ¿Qué le dan a Gabi los extraterrestres?

3. ¿Qué pasa cuando Gabi come?

4. ¿Por qué recuerda todo ahora Gabi?

✓ *Exercise #156*
The sentences below are false. Change each sentence to make it true.

1. Cuando la nave sube en el aire, los extraterrestres duermen y duermen.

2. Gabi escucha el ruido de los extraterrestres.

3. Gabi descubre a los extraterrestres.

4. Los extraterrestres le dan a Gabi un libro extraterrestre.

5. Cuando Gabi come la comida extraterrestre, ella se ríe.

6. Gabi se choca con la puerta de la nave espacial.

119

✓ *Exercise #157*
Choose your favorite episode from #20, #21, #22, #23 or #24 and retell it in the space provided below. Try to add a few extra details that were not given in the original story.

episodio # _____

_____

_____

_____

_____

_____

_____

_____

_____

_____

_____

_____

_____

_____

_____

_____

_____

_____

✓ *Exercise #158*
Create an original story in which the extraterrestrials invite Gabi to visit their planet. Illustrate and narrate your story below.

episodio #25

● ✓ *Exercise #159*
Practice telling episode #25. Use all of the words from the list below.

corren	charlan	el próximo día
(están) emocionados/emocionadas	se divierten	¡No puede ser!
hacen una fiesta	toda la noche	

✓ *Exercise #160*
The sentences below are false. Change each sentence to make it true.

1. Los extraterrestres llevan a Gabi a su planeta.

● 2. Cuando llega la nave espacial, los amigos de Gabi salen de la casa de Gabi.

3. Todos tienen miedo.

4. Invitan al profesor de Marisol y al ladrón a la fiesta.

5. Todos bailan y charlan toda la mañana.

✓ *Exercise #161*
Answer the following questions about episode #25.

1. ¿A dónde van Gabi y los extraterrestres?

2. ¿Por qué están emocionados todos?

3. ¿Qué hacen los amigos de Gabi?

● 4. ¿Quién va a la fiesta?

5. ¿Cuál de los amigos de Gabi no va a la fiesta?

123

✓ *Exercise #162*
Create an original story describing what happens when the maid arrives at Gabi's house the day after the party. Illustrate your new story below.

✓ *Exercise #163*
Narrate below the new story you illustrated in Exercise #162.

vocabulario completo

episodio #1

el lunes	*on Monday*
la gatita	*the (female) kitten*
se llama	*his/her name is*
duerme	*he/she sleeps*
está contento	*he is happy*
está contenta	*she is happy*
el despertador	*the alarm clock*
suena	*it rings*
come	*he/she eats*
¡Qué problema!	*What a problem!*

episodio #2

el martes	*on Tuesday*
la aspiradora	*the vacuum cleaner*
llega	*he/she/it arrives*
la criada	*the maid*
prende	*he/she turns (something) on*
el radio	*the radio (the piece of equipment)*
la radio	*the radio (the music that one hears)*
se duerme	*he/she falls asleep*
otra vez	*again*
¡Qué ruido!	*How noisy!*

episodio #3

el miércoles	*on Wednesday*
la casa	*the house*
está sucio	*he/it is dirty*
está sucia	*she/it is dirty*
limpia	*he/she cleans*
busca	*he/she looks for*
enchufa	*he/she plugs in*
la cola	*the tail*
pasa la aspiradora	*he/she vacuums*
¡Qué lío!	*What a mess!*

episodio #4

el jueves	*on Thursday*
tiene (mucha) hambre	*he/she is (very) hungry*
abre	*he/she opens*
el refrigerador	*the refrigerator*
cierra	*he/she closes*
la puerta	*the door*
el imán	*the magnet*
los imanes	*the magnets*
se pega	*he/she/it sticks to*
¡Qué ridículo!	*How ridiculous!*

episodio #5

la muchacha	*the girl*
la amiga	*the (female) friend*
el amigo	*the (male) friend*
es inteligente	*he/she is smart*
es biencriado	*he is well-behaved*
es biencriada	*she is well-behaved*
el viernes	*on Friday*
el examen	*the test*
la escuela	*the school*
la nariz	*the nose*
¡Qué vergüenza!	*How embarrassing!*

episodio #6

llama por teléfono	*he/she calls on the phone*
llora	*he/she cries*
explica	*he/she explains*
está desesperado	*he is desperate*
está desesperada	*she is desperate*
trota	*he/she jogs*
se pone	*he/she puts (something) on*
el sombrero	*the hat*
la ropa	*the clothes (clothing)*
preferido/preferida	*favorite*
¡Qué engañoso!	*How tricky!*

episodio #7

camina	*he/she walks*
la clase	*the class*
se sienta	*he/she sits down*
el pupitre	*the student desk*
toma	*he/she takes*
engaña	*he/she fools (someone)*
el sábado	*on Saturday*
tiene	*he/she has*
¡Qué travieso!	*How mischievous!*

episodio #8

el domingo	*on Sunday*
el control remoto	*the remote control*
sale	*he/she leaves*
la vecindad	*the neighborhood*
el garaje	*the garage*
los garajes	*the garages*
se apaga	*it turns (itself) off*
apaga	*he/she turns it off*
se apagan	*they turn (themselves) off*
apagan	*they turn it off*
se prenden	*they turn (themselves) on*
se abren	*they open (themselves)*
se cierran	*they close (themselves)*
¡Qué curioso!	*How strange!*

episodio #9

la competencia de belleza	*the beauty contest*
prepara	*he/she prepares (someone or something)*
se prepara	*he/she gets ready*
preparan	*they prepare (someone or something)*
se preparan	*they get ready*
luce	*he/she/it shines*
recita	*he/she recites*
el poema	*the poem*
el juez	*the judge*
los jueces	*the judges*
gana	*he/she wins*
el premio	*the prize*
¡Qué talento!	*What talent!*

episodio #10

el barco de vela	*the sailboat*
hace planes	*he/she makes plans*
hace las maletas	*he/she packs his/her suitcases*
el viaje	*the trip*
está preparado	*he is prepared (he is ready)*
está preparada	*she is prepared (she is ready)*
tiene talento	*he/she has talent*
no tiene talento	*he/she does not have talent*
practica	*he/she practices*
por fin	*finally*
se despide	*he/she says goodbye*
¡Buen viaje!	*Have a good trip!*

episodio #11

navega	*he/she sails (navigates)*
el mar	*the sea*
bucea	*he/she scuba dives*
se choca (con)	*he/she/it crashes (into)*
el tiburón	*the shark*
muerde	*he/she/it bites*
tiene (mucho) miedo	*he/she is (very) scared*
se hunde	*he/she/it sinks*
¡Socorro!	*Help!*

episodio #12

de repente	*suddenly*
el avión	*the airplane*
estornuda	*he/she/it sneezes*
sube	*he/she/it rises (goes up) (climbs)*
vuela	*he/she/it flies*
se cae	*he/she falls down*
la isla	*the island*
¡Qué alivio!	*What a relief!*
¡Qué suerte!	*How lucky! (What luck!)*

episodio #13

está curioso	*he is curious*
está curiosa	*she is curious*
explora	*he/she explores*
el ramo	*the branch*
el árbol	*the tree*
el mono	*the monkey*
se enoja	*he/she gets mad*
¡Dale!	*STEP ON IT!*

episodio #14

encuentra	*he/she finds*
el rey	*the king*
la reina	*the queen*
lleva	*he/she carries*
la cima	*the summit (of a mountain or volcano)*
el volcán	*the volcano*
le da una patada	*he/she kicks (someone)*
hace (mucho) calor	*it is (very) hot*
¡Qué sabroso/sabrosa!	*How tasty!*
¡Qué horror!	*How horrible!*

episodio #15

el esquimal	*the Eskimo*
explota	*it explodes*
vive	*he/she/it lives*
aplasta	*he/she/it smashes*
se ríe	*he/she laughs*
va de caza	*he/she goes hunting*
invita	*he/she invites*
da	*he/she gives*
¡Ojo!	*Watch out!*

episodio #16

va de pesca	*he/she goes fishing*
van de pesca	*they go fishing*
hace (mucho) frío	*it is (very) cold*
el abrigo	*the coat*
la caña de pescar	*the fishing pole*
corta	*he/she cuts*
el hielo	*the ice*
el lago	*the lake*
salva	*he/she saves (someone or something)*
¡Qué desgracia!	*How disgraceful! (What a disgrace!)*

episodio #17

va de vacaciones	*he/she goes on vacation*
la calle	*the street*
el banco	*the bank*
el ladrón	*the thief*
roba	*he/she steals*
la lucha	*the fight*
resulta una lucha	*a fight breaks out*
las monedas	*the coins*
¡Disculpe!	*Excuse me! (Pardon me!)*

episodio #18

se quita	*he/she takes (something) off*
el zapato	*the shoe*
pega	*he/she/it hits*
la policía	*the police*
el policía	*the policeman*
captura	*he/she captures*
el dolor de cabeza	*the headache*
está alarmado	*he is alarmed*
está alarmada	*she is alarmed*
¡Bien se lo merece!	*He/She deserves it!*

episodio #19

la prensa	*the media (the press)*
el fotógrafo	*the (male) photographer*
la fotógrafa	*the (female) photographer*
saca una foto	*he/she takes a picture*
el periodista	*the (male) journalist*
la periodista	*the (female) journalist*
entrevista	*he/she interviews (someone)*
pregunta	*he/she asks*
recuerda	*he/she remembers*
la amnesia	*amnesia*
nada	*nothing*
¡No faltaba más!	*That's all I/we/he/she needed!*

episodio #20

el médico	*the (male) doctor*
la médica	*the (female) doctor*
escucha	*he/she listens to*
el corazón	*the heart*
saca un rayo-equis	*he/she takes an X-ray*
está sorprendido	*he is surprised*
está sorprendida	*she is surprised*
saca	*he/she takes (something) out*
la inyección	*the injection (the shot)*
¡Qué extraño!	*How strange!*
¡Qué dolor!	*How painful!*

135

episodio #21

tiene (mucha) suerte	*he/she is (very) lucky*
conoce	*he/she knows or meets (someone)*
el ballet	*ballet*
el elefante	*the elephant*
es famoso	*he is famous*
es famosa	*she is famous*
baila	*he/she dances*
aprende	*he/she learns*
¡Qué lástima!	*What a shame!*

episodio #22

la nave espacial	*the spaceship*
el extraterrestre/la extraterrestre	*the extraterrestrial*
los extraterrestres	*the extraterrestrials*
es rizado/rizada	*it is curly*
es viscoso/viscosa	*it is slimy*
es feo	*he is ugly*
es fea	*she is ugly*
son feos	*they (masculine) are ugly*
son feas	*they (feminine) are ugly*
hacen un picnic	*they go on a picnic*
el caracol/los caracoles	*the snail/the snails*
está cansado	*he is tired*
está cansada	*she is tired*
están cansados	*they (masculine) are tired*
están cansadas	*they (feminine) are tired*
la comida	*the food*
¡Qué disgusto!	*How disgusting!*

episodio #23

huele	*he/she smells (something)*
no aguanta más	*he/she can't take/stand it any more*
el volumen	*the volume*
se tropieza	*he/she trips*
empuja	*he/she pushes*
se da cuenta	*he/she realizes*
no se da cuenta	*he/she doesn't realize*
¡Qué peligro!	*How dangerous!*
¡Caray!	*Oh, no!*

episodio #24

se despierta	*he/she wakes up*
se despiertan	*they wake up*
el ruido	*the noise*
la cama	*the bed*
descubre	*he/she discovers*
descubren	*they discover*
flota	*he/she/it floats*
el techo	*the ceiling*
¡Increíble!	*Incredible!*

episodio #25

corre	*he/she runs*
corren	*they run*
está emocionado	*he is excited*
está emocionada	*she is excited*
están emocionados	*they (masculine) are excited*
están emocionadas	*they (feminine) are excited*
hace una fiesta	*he/she throws a party*
hacen una fiesta	*they throw a party*
charla	*he/she chats*
charlan	*they chat*
se divierte	*he/she has fun*
se divierten	*they have fun*
toda la noche	*all night long*
el próximo día	*the next day*
¡No puede ser!	*It can't be!*

AST SPA 031505